# About Skill Builders
# Introduction to
# Geometry
## Grades 4–5

Welcome to Skill Builders *Introduction to Geometry* for grades 4–5. This book is designed to improve children's geometry skills through focused practice. This full-color workbook contains grade-level-appropriate activities based on national standards to help ensure that children master basic skills before progressing.

More than 70 pages of activities cover essential geometry skills, such as polygons, congruence and symmetry, and angles. The book's colorful, inviting format, easy-to-follow directions, and clear examples help build children's confidence and make math more accessible and enjoyable.

The Skill Builders series offers workbooks that are perfect for keeping skills sharp during the school year or preparing students for the next grade.

## Credits:
Copy Editor: Beatrice Allen
Layout and Cover Design: Nick Green

www.carsondellosa.
Carson-Dellosa Publishing LLC
Greensboro, North Carolina

D1167029

ISBN 978-1-936023-24-0
03-091131151

# Table of Contents

# Polygons

**Match each polygon with its definition.**

    **H**   is a polygon with six sides.

1. \_\_\_\_\_ is a quadrilateral with opposite sides parallel.

2. \_\_\_\_\_ is a polygon with three angles.

3. \_\_\_\_\_ is an eight-sided polygon.

4. \_\_\_\_\_ is a plane figure with four equal sides and four right angles. Opposite sides are parallel.

5. \_\_\_\_\_ is a five-sided polygon.

6. \_\_\_\_\_ is an irregular polygon.

7. \_\_\_\_\_ is a quadrilateral with four right angles. Opposite sides are parallel, but not all sides are equal.

8. \_\_\_\_\_ is a quadrilateral with only two parallel sides.

A.

B.

C.

D.

E.

F.

G.

H.

I.

# Polygons

Match each polygon with its name.

A.

B.

C.

D.

E.

F.

G.

H.

I.

1. _____ pentagon

2. _____ square

3. _____ rectangle

4. _____ triangle

5. _____ quadrilateral

6. _____ parallelogram

7. _____ hexagon

8. _____ octagon

9. _____ trapezoid

# Polygons

**Match the name of each polygon with its definition.**

A. pentagon      B. parallelogram

C. square      D. hexagon

E. rectangle      F. octagon

G. triangle      H. trapezoid

I. quadrilateral      J. polygon

1. _____ a polygon with six sides

2. _____ a quadrilateral with opposite sides parallel and congruent

3. _____ a polygon with three angles

4. _____ a plane figure in which all of the angles are right angles; opposite sides are parallel, and opposite angles are equal

5. _____ a rectangle with all four sides equal; opposite sides are parallel, and opposite angles are equal

6. _____ a five-sided polygon

7. _____ a figure made up of three or more line segments connected so that the area is closed in

8. _____ an eight-sided polygon

9. _____ any four-sided figure

10. _____ a quadrilateral with two sides not parallel and two sides parallel

# Polygons

**Tell whether the polygon is regular or not. Write *regular* or *not regular*.**

A **polygon** is a closed plane figure with straight sides that is named by the number of its sides and angles. A **regular polygon** has all sides the same length and all angles equal.

_____**regular**_____

1.

_____

2.

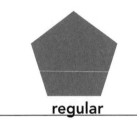

_____

3.

_____

4.

_____

5.

_____

6.

_____

7.

_____

# Polygons

**Draw in the box the polygon that is described.**

This polygon has three equal sides.

This polygon has four equal sides.

This polygon has five equal sides.

This polygon has six equal sides.

This polygon has eight equal sides.

This polygon has 10 equal sides.

# Polygons

**Use the hints to name and draw the polygon.**

| Hint | Polygon Name | Polygon Drawing |
|---|---|---|
| I have four sides. Two are parallel, and two are not parallel. | trapezoid | |
| 1. All four of my sides are equal. | | |
| 2. My opposite sides are equal and parallel. I have four right angles. I am not a square. | | |
| 3. I am a polygon with six sides and six angles. | | |
| 4. I have three sides and three angles. | | |
| 5. I have two right angles and five sides. Two pairs of my sides are perpendicular. | | |

# Polygons

**Solve each problem. Some polygons will be used more than once.**

1. I am a quadrilateral with four congruent sides and no right angles. What am I?

   _____

2. I am a quadrilateral with opposite sides parallel, and I have four right angles. What am I?

   _____

3. I have two pairs of congruent sides and two pairs of parallel sides. Two angles are acute, and two are obtuse. What type of quadrilateral am I?

   _____

4. I have four sides and four angles. Two angles are acute, and two are obtuse. What figure could I be?

   _____

5. Four of my sides are congruent, and I have four right angles. What type of quadrilateral am I?

   _____

6. I am a quadrilateral with opposite sides congruent and two pairs of right angles. What am I?

   _____

# Polygons

**Solve each problem.**

| triangle | parallelogram | trapezoid | hexagon |

What is the fewest number of triangles that make up a parallelogram? _____**2**_____

1. What is the fewest number of triangles that make up a trapezoid? _____

2. What is the fewest number of triangles that make up a hexagon?_____

3. What combination of polygons could you use to make a trapezoid?_____

4. What combination of polygons could you use to make a hexagon?_____

5. Write another combination of polygons that you could use to make a hexagon. _____

# Polygons

Below are signs that you might see in your city. Next to each sign, write the name of the polygon.

1.  _____

2.  _____

3.  _____

4.  _____

5.  _____

# Three-Dimensional Figures

**Match each three-dimensional figure with its name.**

A.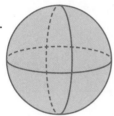

B.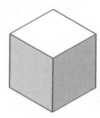

C.

D.

E.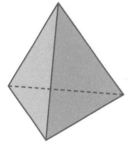

F.

1. _____ rectangular prism

2. _____ cube

3. _____ triangular pyramid

4. _____ sphere

5. _____ cone

6. _____ cylinder

# Three-Dimensional Figures

**Draw each three-dimensional figure.**

cube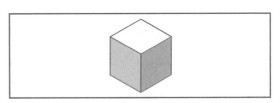

1. cylinder

2. sphere

3. cone

4. rectangular prism

5. triangular pyramid

# Lines, Angles, and Faces

**Match each picture with its name.**

1. _____ parallel lines        2. _____ perpendicular lines

3. _____ vertex                 4. _____ face

5. _____ edge                   6. _____ ray

7. _____ line segment           8. _____ angle

A.

B.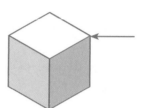

C.

D.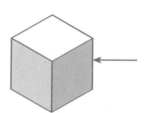

E.

F.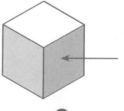

G.

H.

# Lines, Angles, and Faces

**Draw lines to match the names with the definitions.**

1.  parallel lines

lines that never intersect

2.  perpendicular lines

lines that intersect to form four right angles

3.  vertex

a flat surface of a solid figure

4.  face

a line segment where two or more faces of a solid figure meet

5.  edge

the endpoint of three line segments on a solid figure

6.  ray

the space between two nonparallel rays that share an endpoint

7.  line segment

lines that cross each other at only one point

8.  angle

a line with two endpoints

9.  intersecting lines

a line that has one endpoint and continues in one direction

# Perimeter

**Find the perimeter of each polygon.**

To find the **perimeter**, add all of the side lengths of the polygon together.

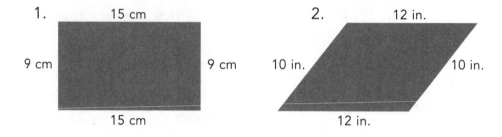

1.
15 cm
9 cm    9 cm
15 cm

2.
12 in.
10 in.    10 in.
12 in.

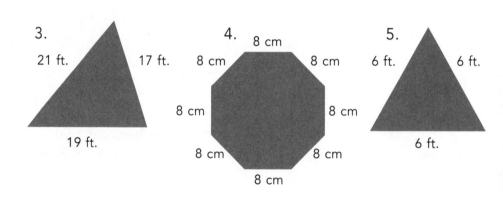

3.
21 ft.    17 ft.
19 ft.

4.
8 cm
8 cm    8 cm
8 cm    8 cm
8 cm    8 cm
8 cm

5.
6 ft.    6 ft.
6 ft.

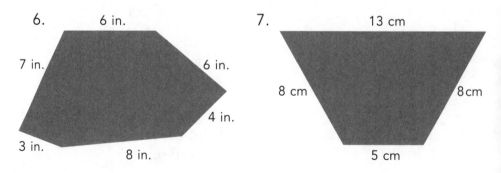

6.
6 in.
7 in.
6 in.
4 in.
3 in.
8 in.

7.
13 cm
8 cm    8 cm
5 cm

# Perimeter

**Find the perimeter of each polygon.**

You can find the perimeter by adding all of the side lengths. You can also use this formula for quadrilaterals with opposite sides equal: P = (2 × L) + (2 × W).

P = (2 × 12) + (2 × 3)
P = 24 + 6
P = 30 in.

3 in.

12 in.

1. P = (2 × _____) + (2 × _____)
   P = _____ + _____
   P = _____

6 in.

6 in.

2. P = (2 × _____) + (2 × _____)
   P = _____ + _____
   P = _____

3 m

15 m

3. P = (2 × _____) + (2 × _____)
   P = _____ + _____
   P = _____

4 in.

1 in.

4. P = (2 × _____) + (2 × _____)
   P = _____ + _____
   P = _____

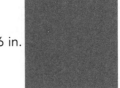

4 mm        4 mm

# Perimeter

Write how many units form the perimeter of each polygon.

| 1 | 2 | 3 | 4 | 5 |
|---|---|---|---|---|
| 16 | | | | 6 |
| 15 | | | | 7 |
| 14 | | | | 8 |
| 13 | 12 | 11 | 10 | 9 |

16 units

1.

_____

2.

_____

3.
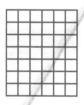

_____

4.

_____

5.
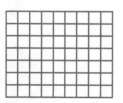

_____

6.
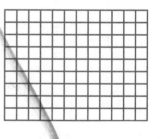

_____

# Perimeter

**Solve each problem.**

1. Mrs. Johansen's pool is a rectangle that is 24 feet long and 13 feet wide. What is the perimeter of her pool?

   The pool's perimeter is _____ feet.

2. The rectangular table is 24 centimeters long and 15 centimeters wide. What is the perimeter of the tabletop?

   The tabletop's perimeter is _____ centimeters.

3. A playground is rectangular. It measures 280 feet long and 124 feet wide. What is the perimeter of the playground?

   The playground's perimeter is _____ feet.

4. The garden is a rectangle. It is 14 meters long and 13 meters wide. How much fencing will it take to go around the garden?

   The garden needs _____ meters of fencing.

5. The rectangular mirror is 28 inches wide and 36 inches long. What is the perimeter of the mirror?

   The mirror's perimeter is _____ inches.

# Perimeter

Find the perimeter of each figure. Write the letter that represents each problem above its answer.

Riddle: Where does the crab spider live?

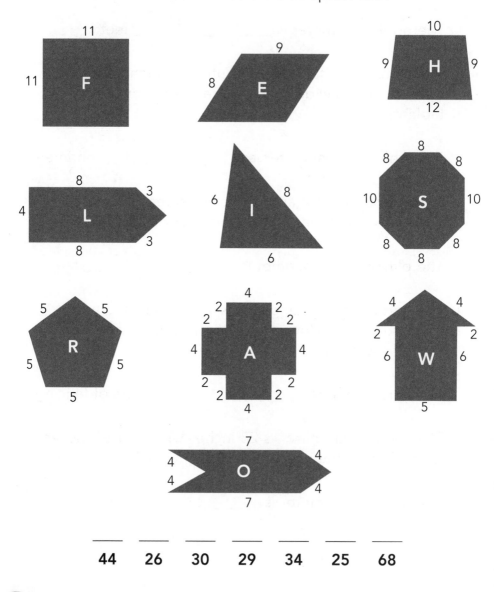

| __ | __ | __ | __ | __ | __ | __ |
|----|----|----|----|----|----|----|
| 44 | 26 | 30 | 29 | 34 | 25 | 68 |

# Area

**Find the area of each figure.**

Area tells the number of square units in a figure.

1.
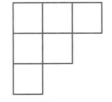

_____ square units

2.
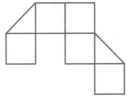

_____ square units

3.

_____ square units

4.
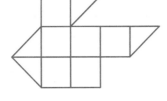

_____ square units

5.
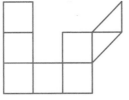

_____ square units

6.
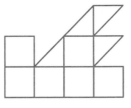

_____ square units

# Area

**Find the area of each figure.**

The **area** is the space inside a figure. To find the area of a regular quadrilateral, multiply its length by its width.

Width: 12 cm

Solve: A = L × W

12 × 12 = **144 cm²**

Length: 12 cm

1.  7 in.

14 in. _____

2.  8 cm

8 cm _____

3.  10 in.

4 in. _____

4. 7 ft.   7 ft. _____

5.  2 in.

9 in. _____

# Area

**Write the area of each room.**

1. bedroom 2 _____      2. master bedroom _____

3. living room _____      4. dining room _____

5. kitchen _____      6. toy room _____

7. What is the largest room? _____

8. What is the smallest room? _____

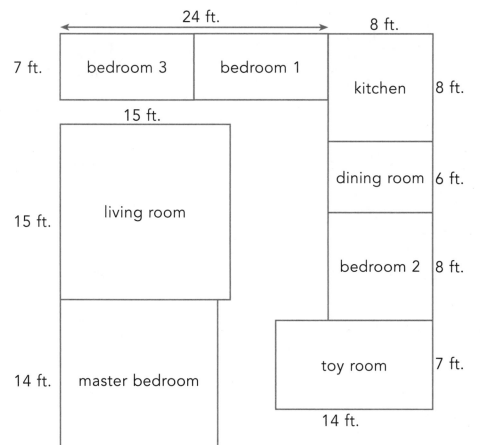

# Area

Solve the riddle by finding the area of each figure. Write the letter that represents each problem above its answer.

Riddle: What state is closest to the equator?

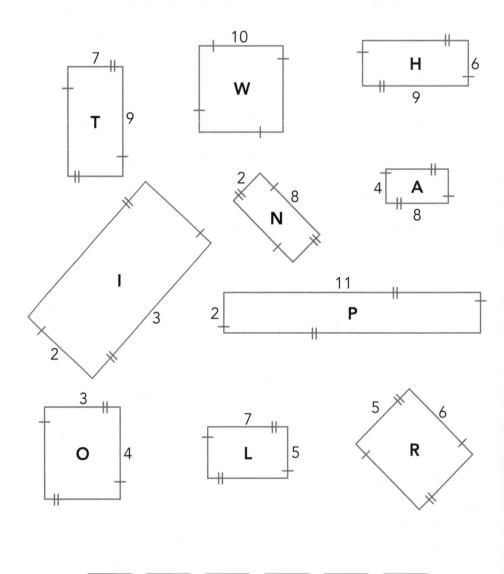

7  **T**  9

10  **W**

**H**  6  9

**N**  2  8

4  **A**  8

**I**  3  2

11  **P**  2

3  **O**  4

7  **L**  5

5  **R**  6

$\overline{\phantom{XX}}$ $\overline{\phantom{XX}}$ $\overline{\phantom{XX}}$ $\overline{\phantom{XX}}$ $\overline{\phantom{XX}}$ $\overline{\phantom{XX}}$
54    32    100    32    6    6

# Circles

**Draw an example for each term.**

**Chord:** a line segment passing through a circle that has its endpoints on that circle

**Circumference:** the distance around a circle

**Diameter:** a chord passing through a circle's center point

**Radius:** a line segment with one endpoint at the center of a circle and the other endpoint on the circle

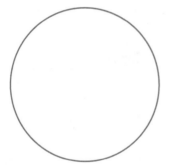

Draw a radius AB.

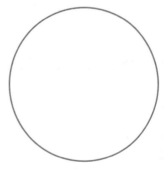

Trace the circumference.

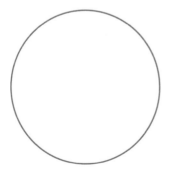

Draw a diameter XY.

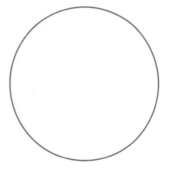

Draw a chord DE.

# Circles

**Solve each problem.**

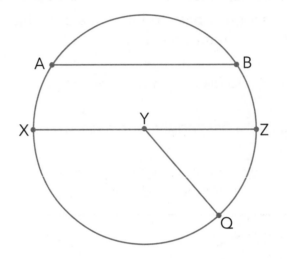

| Name | Part of Circle |
|------|---------------|
| YQ | 1. |
| AB | 2. |
| YZ | 3. |
| XZ | 4. |

5. The center of the circle is _____ .

6. Two points on the circle are _____ and _____ .

# Circles

**Solve each problem.**

**Remember**: A circle is named by its center point.

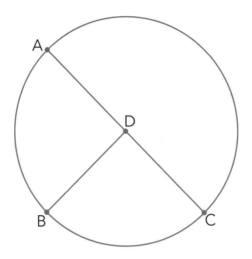

1. What is this circle named? _____

2. Name two radii. _____  _____

3. Name the diameter. _____

4. Draw another diameter in red and name it EF.

5. Draw two more radii in blue and label them DG and DH.

# Circles

**Solve each problem. Show your work.**

**Remember:** The circumference is about 3 times the diameter of a circle. If you know the diameter, you can estimate the circumference.

$C \approx 3 \times$ diameter

Diameter = 6 cm

$6 \times 3 = 18$

**Circumference ≈ 18 cm**

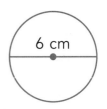

6 cm

1. Diameter = 4 in.

   _____ × _____ =

   The circumference is about _____.

   4 in.

2. Diameter = 9 yd.

   _____ × _____ =

   The circumference is about _____.

   9 yd.

3. Diameter = 12 mm

   _____ × _____ =

   The circumference is about _____.

   12 mm

4. Diameter = 8 ft.

   _____ × _____ =

   The circumference is about _____.

   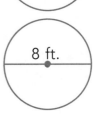

   8 ft.

# Circles

**Solve each problem. Show your work.**

**Remember**: The radius is half the diameter of a circle. To find the diameter, double the radius.

Find the diameter.

radius × 2 = diameter

4 × 2 = 8

**diameter = 8 in.**

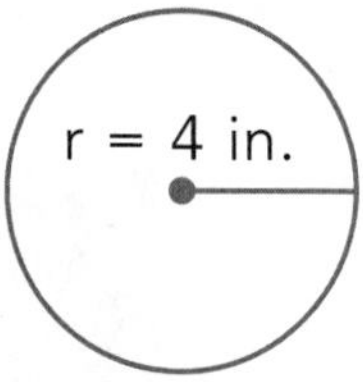

r = 4 in.

1. Find the diameter.

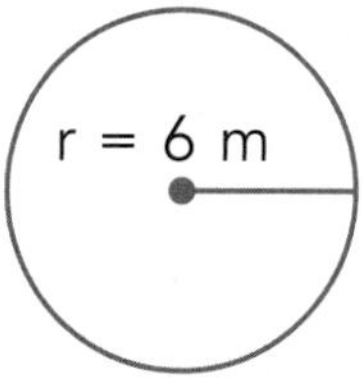

r = 6 m

2. Find the diameter.

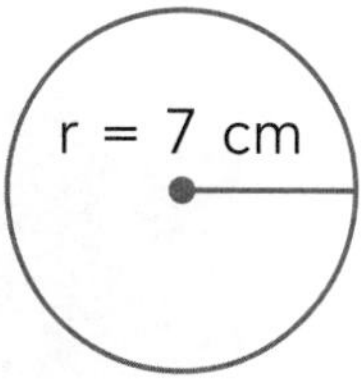

r = 7 cm

3. Find the radius.

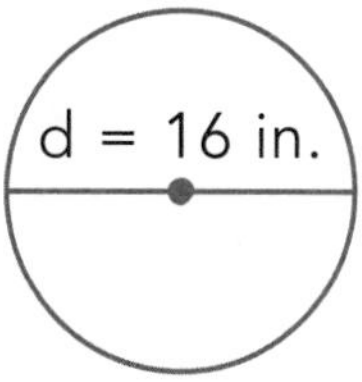

d = 16 in.

4. Find the radius.

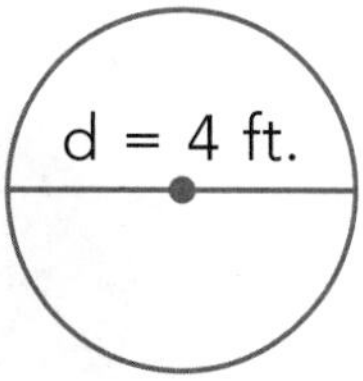

d = 4 ft.

5. Find the radius.

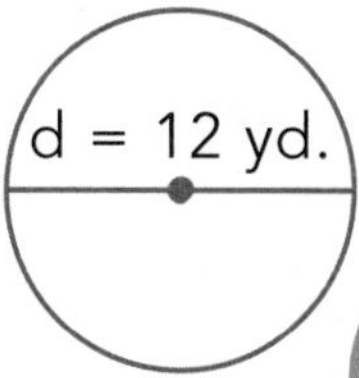

d = 12 yd.

# Symmetry and Congruence

Write how many lines of symmetry each figure has. Then, draw the lines of symmetry.

A **line of symmetry** divides a figure into two congruent figures. **Congruent** figures are identical.

1.

_____

2.

_____

3.

_____

4.

_____

5.

_____

6.

_____

# Symmetry and Congruence

Complete each design to show symmetry.

1.

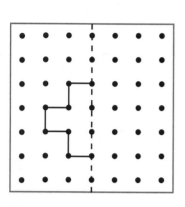

2.

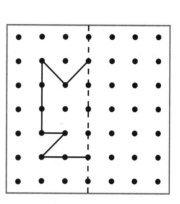

3.

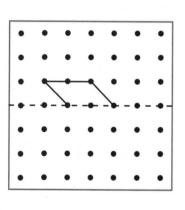

4.

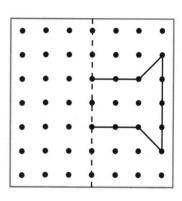

5.

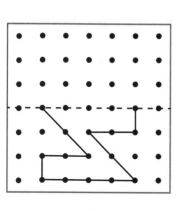

6.

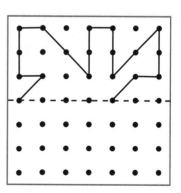

# Symmetry and Congruence

**Color the figures that have the correct line of symmetry.**

**Remember**: A line of symmetry divides a figure into two congruent figures.

1.

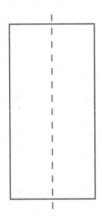

2.

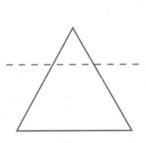

3.

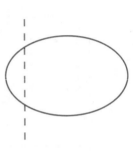

4.

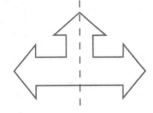

5.

6.

**Draw your own figures with a correct line of symmetry.**

7.

8.

9.

# Transformations

Write how each figure was moved. Write *rotation*, *reflection*, or *translation*.

> **Rotation:** rotates a figure around a point
>
> **Reflection:** flips a figure over a line, making a mirror image
>
> **Translation:** moves a figure to a new position without rotating or reflecting it

1.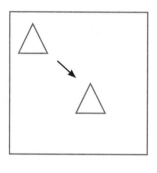

_____

2.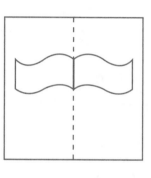

_____

3.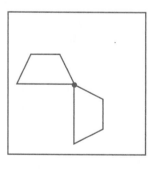

_____

4.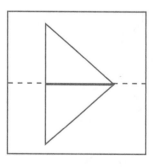

_____

# Congruence

Circle the two figures that are congruent.

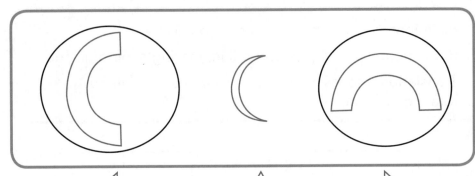

1. A. B. C.

2. A. B. C.

3. A. B. C.

4. A.  B. C.

5. A. B.   C.

# Congruent and Similar Polygons

Label which polygons are congruent and which are similar.
*Congruent* polygons are the exact same shape and size.
*Similar* polygons are the same shape, but not the same size.

1.     2.

_____    _____

Draw a congruent polygon.

3.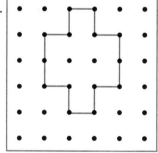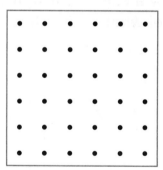

# Transformations

**Draw each figure using either a reflection, translation, or rotation.**

Draw a reflection.

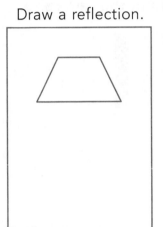

Draw a translation.

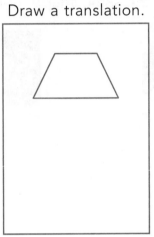

Draw a rotation.

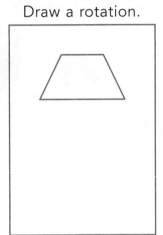

**Draw a congruent figure to each figure already drawn. Label whether it is a reflection, translation, or rotation.**

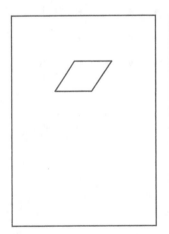

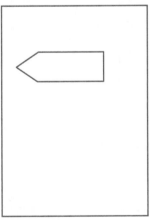

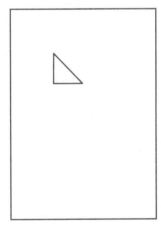

_____    _____    _____

# Transformations

Write how each object was moved. Write *translation*, *rotation*, or *reflection*.

1.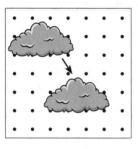

_____

2.

_____

3.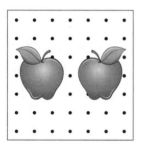

_____

4.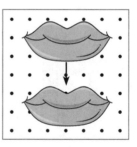

_____

5.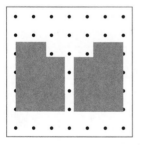

_____

6.

_____

# Volume

**Write the number of cubic units in each figure.**

Volume is the number of cubic units inside a figure.

1.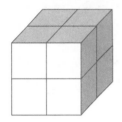

_____ cubic units

2.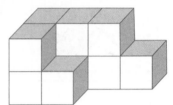

_____ cubic units

3.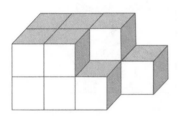

_____ cubic units

4.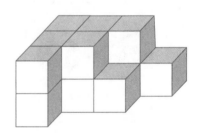

_____ cubic units

5.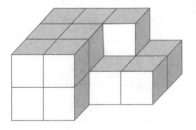

_____ cubic units

6.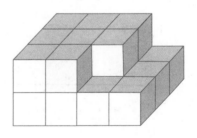

_____ cubic units

# Volume

**Write the volume of each figure.**

length × width × height = volume of a rectangular prism

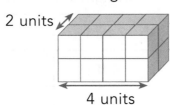

2 units

2 units

4 × 2 × 2 = **16** cubic units

4 units

1.

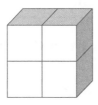

_____ × _____ × _____ = _____

2.

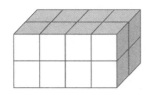

_____ × _____ × _____ = _____

3.

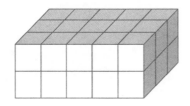

_____ × _____ × _____ = _____

# Volume

**Complete the table.**

| | Length | × | Width | × | Height | = | Volume |
|---|---|---|---|---|---|---|---|
| 1. | 6 mm | | 5 mm | | 2 mm | | |
| 2. | 3 ft. | | 2 ft. | | 4 ft. | | |
| 3. | 10 yd. | | 3 yd. | | 7 yd. | | |
| 4. | 6 cm | | 8 cm | | 9 cm | | |

**Draw and label two rectangular prisms from the table above.**

5. (prism #1)

6. (prism #2)

# Volume

**Find the volume of each figure.**

1.

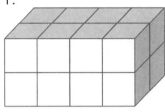

_____ cubic units

2.

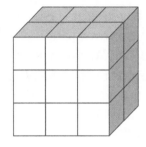

_____ cubic units

3.

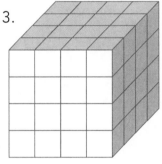

_____ cubic units

4.

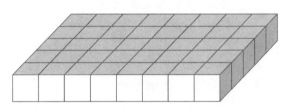

_____ cubic units

5.

_____ cubic units

6.

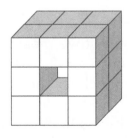

_____ cubic units

# Volume

**Solve each problem. Show your work in the boxes.**

1. A toy box measures 24 centimeters × 18 centimeters × 36 centimeters. What is the volume of the toy box?

2. Dad is building a new sandbox. It measures 12 feet × 1 foot × 6 feet. How much sand does he need to fill the sandbox?

3. The shed in the Peterson's yard is 6 yards × 3 yards × 5 yards. How much space is in the shed?

4. A new stove measures 18 inches × 20 inches × 36 inches. The space for the stove in the kitchen is 5,550 cubic inches. Will the new stove fit? Explain your answer.

_____

_____

_____

# Angles

## Identify each angle.

> **Right Angle:** angle that measures 90 degrees (the angle forms a square corner)
>
> **Acute Angle:** angle that measures less than a right angle, or less than 90 degrees
>
> **Obtuse Angle:** angle that measures more than a right angle, or more than 90 degrees

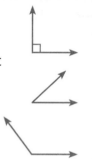

1.

_____

2.

_____

3.

_____

4.

_____

5.

_____

6.

_____

7.

_____

8.

_____

9.

_____

# Angles

Label each figure according to the angles that they contain. Write *acute*, *right*, or *obtuse*. Some may have more than one answer.

1.

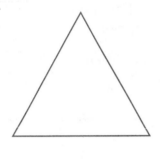

_____

2.

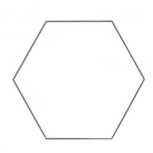

_____

3.

_____

4.

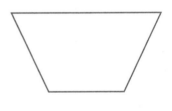

_____

5.

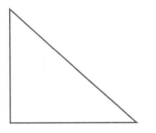

_____

6.

_____

# Angles

Label the angle of each triangle. Write *acute*, *right*, or *obtuse*.

1.

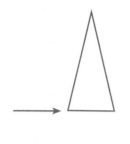

_____

2.

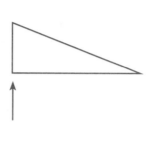

_____

3.

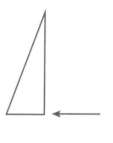

_____

4.

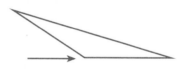

_____

5.

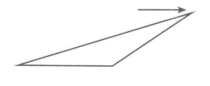

_____

6.

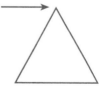

_____

# Angles

**Label each angle.**

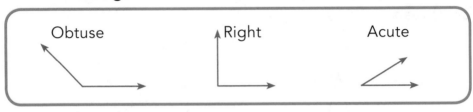

Obtuse        Right        Acute

1.

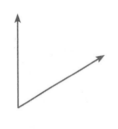

_____

2.

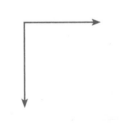

_____

3.

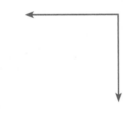

_____

4.

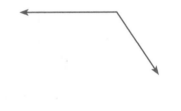

_____

5.

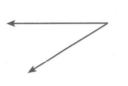

_____

6.

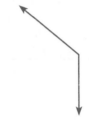

_____

# Angles

**Solve each problem.**

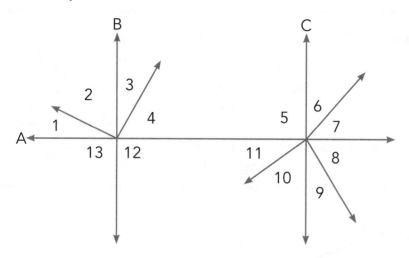

1. Name a pair of parallel lines. _____

2. Name four acute angles. _____

3. When combined, which pairs of angles form a right angle?

   _____

4. Name a pair of perpendicular lines. _____

5. Angle 10 is an _____ angle.

6. Angle 1 is an _____ angle.

7. Angle 8 is an _____ angle.

8. Line A is perpendicular to line _____.

9. Angles 8 and 9 make a _____ angle.

# Angles

**Solve each problem.**

Two rays with the same endpoint form an **angle**.
The endpoint is called the **vertex**.

Write the angle: ∠ **XYZ**
∠ **ZYX**

Read the angle: **Angle XYZ**
**Angle ZYX**

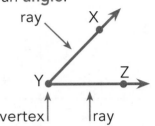

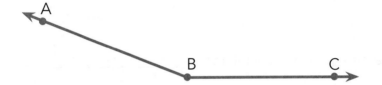

1. List two ways to write this angle. _____

2. Name the two rays. _____

3. Name the vertex. _____

4. What type of angle is this? _____

5. The endpoints of two rays meet at a _____ .

# Lines and Angles

**Draw and label each part.**

1. ray XY

2. obtuse angle LMN

3. line segment PQ

4. right angle XYZ

5. point G

6. line ST

7. acute angle ABC

8. vertex P

# Triangles

**Label each triangle. Write *equilateral, isosceles,* or *scalene*.**

> **Equilateral Triangle:** has three congruent sides
>
> **Isosceles Triangle:** has only two congruent sides
>
> **Scalene Triangle:** has no congruent sides

1.

_____

2.

_____

3.

_____

4.

_____

5.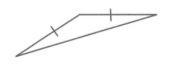

_____

6.

_____

7.

_____

8.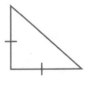

_____

# Triangles

**Identify each triangle. Write *equilateral*, *isosceles*, or *scalene*.**

1. 23 mm, 23 mm, 23 mm

   _____

2. 19 ft., 6 ft., 15 ft.

   _____

3. 29 cm, 3 cm, 27 cm

   _____

4. 15 yd., 7 yd., 15 yd.

   _____

5. 17 in., 17 in., 17 in.

   _____

6. 9 mm, 9 mm, 4 mm

   _____

7. 76 cm, 70 cm, 76 cm

   _____

8. 29 yd., 28 yd., 6 yd.

   _____

# Three-Dimensional Figures

Complete the table.

| Figure | Name | Number of Faces | Number of Edges | Number of Vertices |
|---|---|---|---|---|
| | Triangular Prism | | | |
| | Triangular Pyramid | | | |
| | Square Pyramid | | | |

## Name the figures described below.

1. 9 edges _____

2. 5 vertices _____

3. 4 faces _____

4. 6 vertices _____

5. 4 vertices _____

6. 8 edges _____

7. 5 faces _____

8. 6 edges _____

# Angles

Identify the unknown angle for each triangle. Show your work.

**Remember:** The sum of the angles in a triangle is 180 degrees.

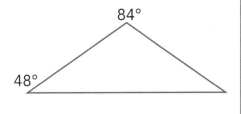
84°

48°

$$\begin{array}{r} \overset{1}{8}4 \\ +\ 48 \\ \hline 132 \end{array} \qquad \begin{array}{r} {}^{7\ 1}1\cancel{8}0 \\ -\ 132 \\ \hline 48 \end{array}$$

missing angle = 48 degrees

1.

90°     45°

2.

75°   90°

3.

60°     60°

# Triangles

**Solve each problem. Write *scalene, isosceles, equilateral,* or *right.***

1. I have three sides and three angles. Only two angles are acute. What kinds of triangles could I be?

   _____

2. I am a triangle with two sides that are the same length. The angles opposite the equal sides are equal. What type of triangle am I?

   _____

3. I am a triangle with no angles the same and no sides the same length. What type of triangle am I?

   _____

4. I am a triangle with all three angles less than a right angle. What types of triangles could I be?

   _____

5. I am a triangle with all three sides equal and all three angles equal. What type of triangle am I?

   _____

6. I am a triangle with one angle larger than ninety degrees. What types of triangles could I be?

   _____

7. I am a triangle with one angle measuring ninety degrees. What type of triangle am I?

   _____

# Coordinate Graphing

Complete the ordered pair so that the missing number is two less than the second number. Then, graph each ordered pair.

> **Example:** ( _____, 7) becomes (5, 7)

1. (_____, 10)

2. (_____, 5)

3. (_____, 9)

4. (_____, 3)

5. (_____, 6)

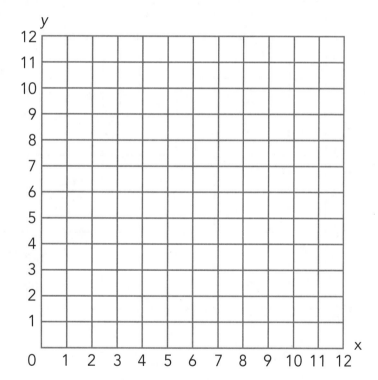

6. (_____, 8)

# Coordinate Graphing

**Tell what food is at each coordinate. Remember to start with the x-axis first.**

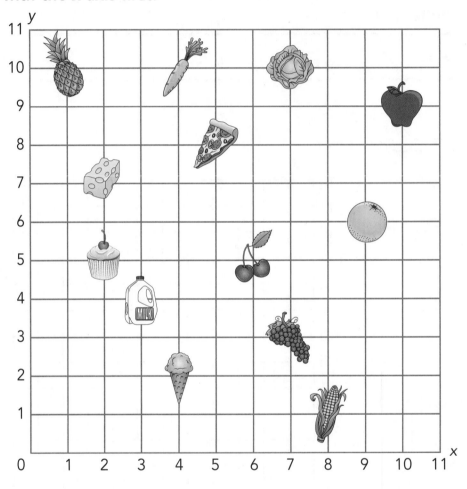

1. (7,3) _____
2. (2,5) _____
3. (3,4) _____
4. (1,10) _____
5. (4,2) _____
6. (10,9) _____
7. (8,1) _____
8. (5,8) _____
9. (9,6) _____
10. (2,7) _____

# Coordinate Graphing

Plot each of the ordered pairs. Then, draw a line connecting the two coordinates. Connect all of the coordinate pairs in order to create half of an arrow. When you are finished, draw the mirror image of the left side of the arrow.

(E,1) ⟶ (D,1)

(D,1) ⟶ (C,1)

(C,1) ⟶ (C,2)

(C,2) ⟶ (C,3)

(C,3) ⟶ (C,4)

(C,4) ⟶ (C,5)

(C,5) ⟶ (C,6)

(C,6) ⟶ (C,7)

(C,7) ⟶ (B,7)

(B,7) ⟶ (A,7)

(A,7) ⟶ (B,8)

(B,8) ⟶ (C,9)

(C,9) ⟶ (D,10)

(D,10) ⟶ (E,11)

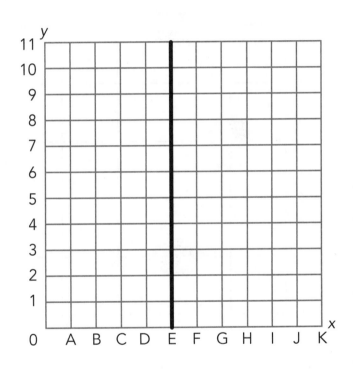

# Coordinate Graphing

Locate the following places on the grid and write the coordinates.

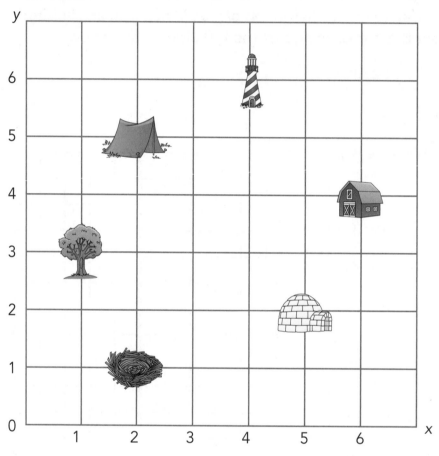

|  | x  y |  | x  y |
|---|---|---|---|
| 1. igloo | (___,___) | 2. nest | (___,___) |
| 3. barn | (___,___) | 4. tent | (___,___) |
| 5. tree | (___,___) | 6. lighthouse | (___,___) |

# Sorting Polygons

Sort the polygons in the Venn diagram.

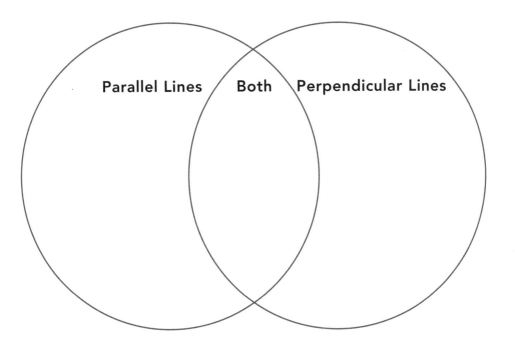

**Parallel Lines**      **Both**      **Perpendicular Lines**

### Word Bank

parallelogram        rectangle

octagon              square

hexagon              pentagon

right triangle

# Regular and Irregular Polygons

**Write the number of each polygon in the correct circle.**

A: Regular Polygons          B: Irregular Polygons

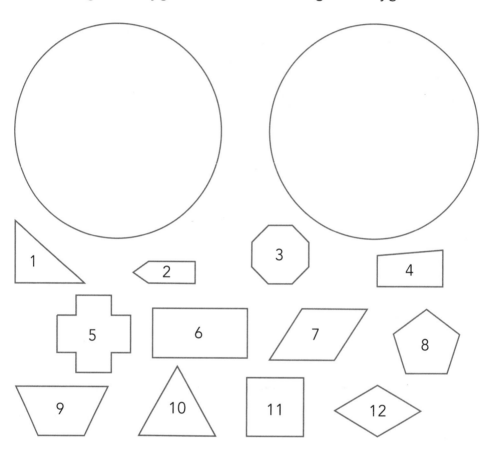

13. Describe the polygons in circle A.

_____

_____

_____

14. Describe the polygons in circle B.

_____

_____

_____

# Congruent Sides

**Write the number of each polygon in the correct circle.**

A: With Four or More
Congruent Sides

B: Without Four
Congruent Sides

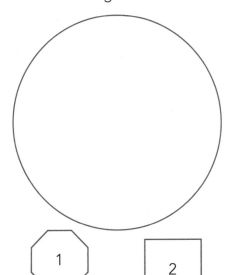

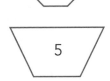

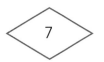

8. Describe the polygons in circle A.

_____

_____

_____

9. Describe the polygons in circle B.

_____

_____

_____

# Triangle Venn Diagram

Describe how acute angles and equilateral triangles are related in the Venn diagram.

**Remember**: An equilateral triangle has congruent sides and angles.

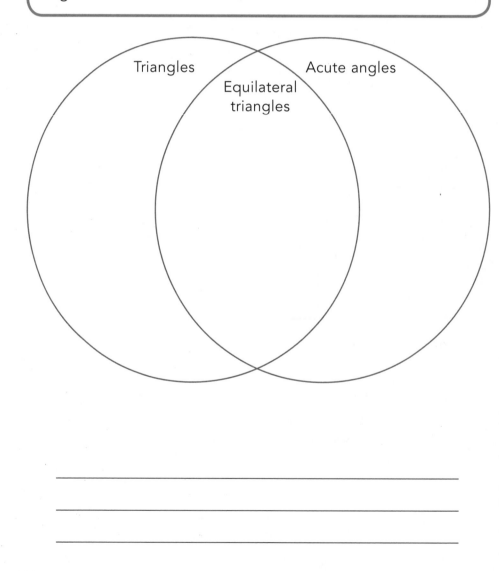

_____

_____

_____

_____

# Coordinate Graphing

**Use the grid to answer the questions.**

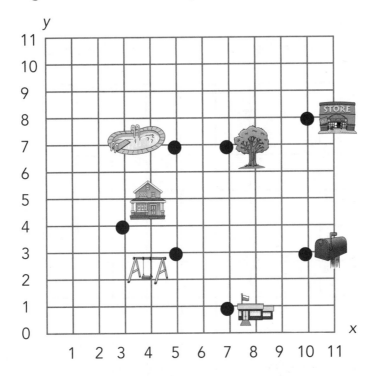

1.  What are the coordinates for the playground? _____

2.  What are the coordinates for the school?  _____

3.  What are the coordinates for your house? _____

4.  Your mom had you do an errand before you could go swimming. She sent you to (10,8). Where did your mom need you to go? _____

5.  Your favorite places are the tree and the pool. What are their coordinates? _____ and _____

# Coordinate Graphing

Solve the riddle by identifying the ordered pair for each letter.

Riddle: What is the lowest point in the United States?

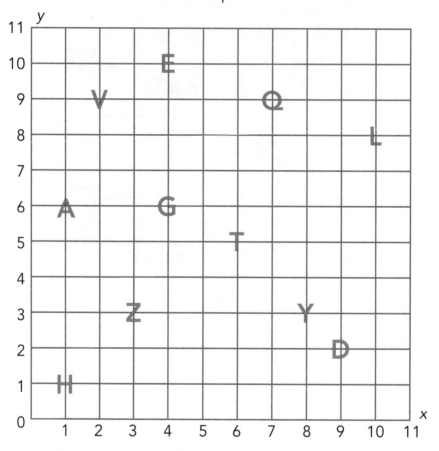

___ ___ ___ ___ ___       ___ ___ ___ ___ ___ ___
(9,2) (4,10) (1,6) (6,5) (1,1)      (2,9) (1,6) (10,8) (10,8) (4,10) (8,3)

# Draw the Object

Draw each object using the directions and the polygons. You may change the size or rotate the polygons as needed.

**Example:**

Draw a tree using 2 triangles and 1 rectangle.

| Draw an ice cream cone using 1 triangle and 3 circles. | Draw a train using 1 triangle, 1 rectangle, and 3 circles. |
|---|---|
| Draw a house using 1 pentagon, 1 rectangle, 2 squares, and 1 circle. | Draw a robot using 1 octagon, 3 ovals, 4 rectangles, and 1 square. |

# Polygon Problem Solving

**Solve each problem.**

1.  Marty said that he drew a triangle with two right angles. Describe and correct his error.

    _____

    _____

    _____

    _____

2.  The radius of Kyle's circle is 18 inches. The diameter of Tyler's circle is 36 inches. Tyler says that his circle is bigger. Describe and correct his error.

    _____

    _____

    _____

    _____

3.  Katelyn said that all of the angles in an octagon are acute. Describe and correct her error.

    _____

    _____

    _____

    _____

# Polygons

Find four different ways to make a polygon that touches four dots but has no dots inside. Each polygon should be different (not congruent).

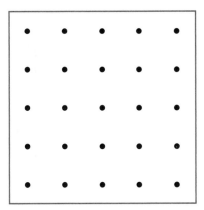

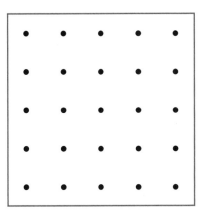

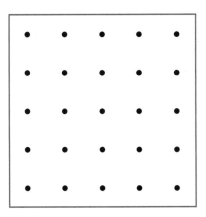

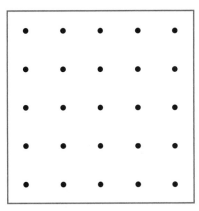

# Word Search

Use the definitions at the bottom to find the names of the polygons in the word search.

| s | l | h | j | r | x | x | q | y | h | d | q | w | c |
|---|---|---|---|---|---|---|---|---|---|---|---|---|---|
| n | i | u | e | e | n | d | o | t | r | o | u | x | t |
| o | o | l | l | c | o | n | g | s | b | p | a | t | o |
| g | s | r | g | t | g | o | b | q | s | j | d | j | z |
| a | e | q | n | a | y | g | u | u | c | r | r | m | x |
| x | c | c | a | n | l | a | q | a | w | x | i | y | w |
| e | v | f | i | g | o | t | g | r | a | g | l | u | f |
| h | f | f | r | l | p | n | c | e | i | f | a | w | e |
| h | h | g | t | e | g | e | r | o | n | v | t | r | z |
| i | x | e | m | a | c | p | n | h | l | m | e | b | k |
| z | r | t | r | a | p | e | z | o | i | d | r | l | x |
| a | z | z | y | f | v | m | v | h | f | u | a | w | h |
| z | k | d | p | k | t | c | t | h | w | i | l | t | i |
| l | p | q | e | v | i | n | h | y | z | v | s | v | j |

1.  a polygon with six sides and six angles _____

2.  a polygon with three angles_____

3.  a plane figure in which all angles are right angles and opposite sides are parallel _____

4.  a five-sided polygon _____

5.  a rectangle with all four sides equal_____

6.  three or more line segments connected so that an area is enclosed inside a figure _____

7.  a quadrilateral with two sides not parallel and two sides parallel _____

# Three-Dimensional Figures

**Identify each figure.**

1.

_____

2.

_____

3.

_____

4.

_____

5.

_____

6.

_____

7.  Describe the figure below using geometric vocabulary (like vertex, face, edge, sphere, cylinder, cube, cone, square pyramid).

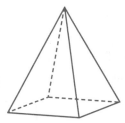

_____

_____

_____

_____

_____

8.  Look at the figures on side A and side B. Write two things that you notice about the figures on side A compared to side B.

_____

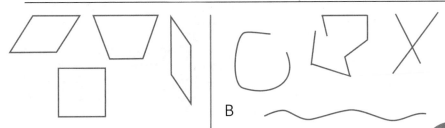

A                                    B

# Classroom Figures

Find and circle these figures in the picture:
13 squares, 3 rectangles, 16 circles, 4 triangles,
3 pentagons, and 2 trapezoids.

9 - 3 =

6 + 3 =

# Lines and Polygons Crossword Puzzle

**Use the definitions to complete the puzzle.**

### Across

1. It has three sides and three angles.

3. It is made up of three or more line segments connected so that the area is closed in.

5. They always have four sides.

8. It has four sides. Opposite angles are the same size.

### Down

2. It has pairs of opposite sides that are parallel, and all sides are congruent.

4. It has four equal sides and four right angles.

6. It has four right angles and two pairs of equal sides, each pair a different length.

7. It has one pair of opposite sides that are parallel, but not equal.

# Puzzling Pieces

**Answer each question.**

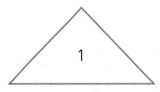 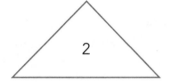 

1. Identify which of the seven figures above will form a square when put together.

_____

_____

2. Which figures would not form a square? Explain why.

_____

_____

_____

# Answer Key

## Page 3
1. D; 2. A; 3. E; 4. F; 5. I; 6. C; 7. G; 8. B

## Page 4
1. H; 2. C; 3. A; 4. I; 5. F; 6. B; 7. E; 8. D; 9. G

## Page 5
1. D; 2. B; 3. G; 4. E; 5. C; 6. A; 7. J; 8. F; 9. I; 10. H

## Page 6
1. regular; 2. not regular; 3. not regular; 4. not regular; 5. regular; 6. regular; 7. not regular

## Page 7

This polygon has three equal sides.

This polygon has four equal sides.

This polygon has five equal sides.

This polygon has six equal sides

This polygon has eight equal sides.

This polygon has 10 equal sides.

## Page 8

| Hint | Polygon Name | Polygon Drawing |
|---|---|---|
| I have four sides. Two are parallel, and two are not parallel. | trapezoid | |
| 1. All four of my sides are equal. | square | |
| 2. My opposite sides are equal and parallel. I have four right angles. I am not a square. | rectangle | |
| 3. I am a polygon with six sides and six angles. | hexagon | |
| 4. I have three sides and three angles. | triangle | |
| 5. I have two pairs of perpendicular lines, two right angles, and five sides. | pentagon | |

## Page 9
Answers will vary but may include:
1. parallelogram, rhombus;
2. square, rectangle;
3. parallelogram; 4. rhombus, trapezoid; 5. square;
6. rectangle

## Page 10
1. 2 triangles; 2. 4 triangles;
3. parallelogram and triangle OR three triangles; 4. 2 trapezoids OR 1 trapezoid and three triangles OR 1 trapezoid, 1 triangle, and 1 parallelogram OR 2 parallelograms and 2 triangles OR 6 triangles;
5. 2 trapezoids OR 1 trapezoid and three triangles OR 1 trapezoid, 1 triangle, and 1 parallelogram OR 2 parallelograms and 2 triangles OR 6 triangles

# Answer Key

## Page 11
1. octagon; 2. triangle; 3. rhombus;
4. triangle; 5. rectangle

## Page 12
1. D; 2. B; 3. E; 4. A; 5. C; 6. F

## Page 13

1. cylinder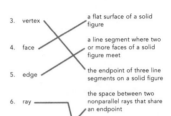

2. sphere

3. cone

4. rectangular prism

5. triangular pyramid

## Page 14
1. A; 2. C; 3. B; 4. F; 5. D; 6. E; 7. H;
8. G

## Page 15

1. parallel lines ——— lines that never intersect

2. perpendicular lines — lines that intersect to form four right angles

3. vertex — a flat surface of a solid figure

4. face — a line segment where two or more faces of a solid figure meet

5. edge — the endpoint of three line segments on a solid figure

6. ray — the space between two nonparallel rays that share an endpoint

7. line segment — lines that cross each other at only one point

8. angle — a line with two endpoints

9. intersecting lines — a line that has one endpoint and continues on in one direction

## Page 16
1. 48 cm; 2. 44 in.; 3. 57 ft.; 4. 64 cm;
5. 18 ft.; 6. 34 in.; 7. 34 cm

## Page 17
1. 24 in.; 2. 36 m; 3. 10 in.; 4. 16 mm

## Page 18
1. 20 units; 2. 18 units; 3. 22 units;
4. 20 units; 5. 28 units; 6. 38 units

## Page 19
1. 74 ft.; 2. 78 cm.; 3. 808 ft.; 4. 54 m;
5. 128 in.

## Page 20
Flowers

## Page 21
1. 6 square units; 2. 6 square units;
3. 7 square units; 4. 8 square units;
5. 7 square units; 6. 8 square units

# Answer Key

## Page 22
1. 98 in.; 2. 64 cm; 3. 40 in.; 4. 49 ft.;
5. 18 in.

## Page 23
1. 64 ft.²; 2. 196 ft.²; 3. 225 ft.²;
4. 48 ft.²; 5. 64 ft.²; 6. 98 ft.²;
7. living room; 8. dining room

## Page 24
Hawaii

## Page 25

Draw a radius AB.    Trace the circumference.

Draw a diameter XY.    Draw a chord DE.

## Page 26
1. radius; 2. chord; 3. radius;
4. diameter; 5. Y; 6. A,B or X,Z

## Page 27
1. D; 2. DA, DC, DB; 3. AC;
4. Answers may vary. A red chord
drawn through the center of the
circle.; 5. Answers may vary. Two
blue line segments with one
endpoint at the center and the other
endpoint on the circle.

## Page 28
1. 12 in.; 2. 27 yd.; 3. 36 mm; 4. 24 ft.

## Page 29
1. 12 m; 2. 14 cm; 3. 8 in.; 4. 2 ft.;
5. 6 yd.

## Page 30
1. 4 or more lines of symmetry;
2. 1 line of symmetry; 3. no line of
symmetry; 4. 2 lines of symmetry;
5. 1 line of symmetry;
6. no line of symmetry

## Page 31
1. 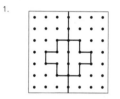 2.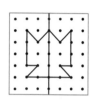

3. 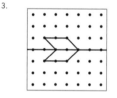 4.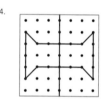

5. 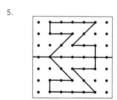 6.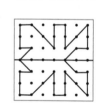

## Page 32
1, 4, 5, 6 are correct lines of
symmetry and should be colored.
7, 8, 9, should demonstrate any
figure or design with a correct line of
symmetry.

## Page 33
1. translation; 2. reflection;
3. rotation; 4. reflection

# Answer Key

## Page 34
1. A,C; 2. A,B; 3. A,C; 4. A,B; 5. B,C

## Page 35
1. congruent; 2. similar; 3. image should be identical (the same size and shape)

## Page 36

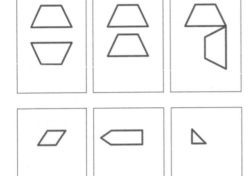

## Answers Will Vary

## Page 37
1. translation; 2. rotation;
3. reflection; 4. translation;
5. reflection; 6. translation

## Page 38
1. 8 cubic units; 2. 10 cubic units;
3. 12 cubic units; 4. 14 cubic units;
5. 17 cubic units; 6. 20 cubic units

## Page 39
1. 4 cubic units; 2. 16 cubic units;
3. 30 cubic units

## Page 40
1. 60 mm$^3$; 2. 24 ft.$^3$; 3. 210 yd.$^3$;
4. 432 cm$^3$; 5.–6. Drawings will vary.

## Page 41
1. 16; 2. 18; 3. 64; 4. 40; 5. 12; 6. 16

## Page 42
1. 15,552 cm$^3$; 2. 72 ft.$^3$; 3. 90 yd.$^3$;
4. No, the new stove will not fit because it measures 12,960 in.$^3$.

## Page 43
1. right; 2. obtuse; 3. acute;
4. obtuse; 5. acute; 6. right;
7. acute; 8. obtuse; 9. right

## Page 44
1. acute; 2. obtuse; 3. right;
4. obtuse, acute; 5. right, acute;
6. right

## Page 45
1. acute; 2. right; 3. right; 4. obtuse;
5. acute; 6. acute

## Page 46
1. acute; 2. obtuse; 3. right;
4. obtuse; 5. acute; 6. right

## Page 47
1. B, C; 2. 1, 2, 3, 4, 6, 7, 8, 9, 10, 11 (any four); 3. 1, 2; 3, 4; 6, 7; 8, 9; 10, 11; 4. AB, AC; 5. acute; 6. acute;
7. acute; 8. B or C; 9. right

# Answer Key

## Page 48
1. angle ABC; angle CBA; 2. $\overrightarrow{BC}$, $\overrightarrow{BA}$;
3. B; 4. obtuse; 5. vertex

## Page 49
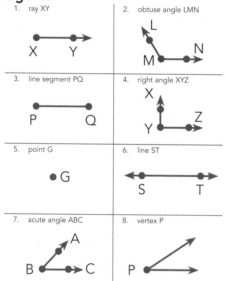

1. ray XY
2. obtuse angle LMN
3. line segment PQ
4. right angle XYZ
5. point G
6. line ST
7. acute angle ABC
8. vertex P

## Page 50
1. isosceles; 2. scalene;
3. equilateral; 4. scalene;
5. isosceles; 6. equilateral;
7. isosceles; 8. isosceles

## Page 51
1. equilateral; 2. scalene; 3. scalene;
4. isosceles; 5. equilateral;
6. isosceles; 7. isosceles; 8. scalene

## Page 52

| Figure | Name | Number of Faces | Number of Edges | Number of Vertices |
|---|---|---|---|---|
| | Triangular Prism | 5 | 9 | 6 |
| | Triangular Pyramid | 4 | 6 | 4 |
| | Square Prism | 5 | 8 | 5 |

1. triangular prism; 2. square
pyramid; 3. triangular pyramid;
4. triangular prism; 5. triangular
pyramid; 6. square pyramid;
7. triangular prism/square pyramid;
8. triangular pyramid

## Page 53
1. 48°; 2. 45°; 3. 15°; 4. 60°

## Page 54
1. scalene or isosceles; 2. isosceles;
3. scalene; 4. equilateral, scalene, or
isosceles; 5. equilateral; 6. scalene or
isosceles; 7. right

## Page 55
1. 8; 2. 3; 3. 7; 4. 1; 5. 4; 6. 6

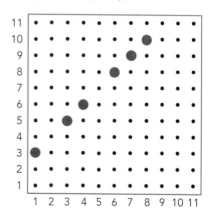

# Answer Key

## Page 56
1. grapes; 2. cupcake; 3. milk;
4. pineapple; 5. ice-cream cone;
6. apple; 7. corn; 8. pizza;
9. orange; 10. cheese

## Page 57
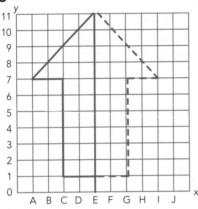

## Page 58
1. ( 5,2); 2. (2,1); 3. (6,4); 4. (2,5);
5. (1,3); 6. (4,6)

## Page 59
Parallel Lines: hexagon,
parallelogram, octagon;
Perpendicular Lines: right triangle
Both: pentagon, rectangle, square

## Page 60
Regular polygons include: 3, 8, 10,
11. Irregular Polygons include: 1, 2,
4, 5, 6, 7, 9, 12.; 13. All figures have
sides that are equal lengths and
have equal angles.; 14. All sides and
angles are not the same size.

## Page 61
With: 1, 2, 4, 7; Without: 3, 5, 6;
8. All sides are equal.; 9. All sides are
not equal.

## Page 62
All equilateral triangles have three
acute angles.

## Page 63
1. (5,3); 2. (7,1); 3. (3,4); 4. store;
5. (7,7) and (5,7)

## Page 64
Death Valley

## Page 65
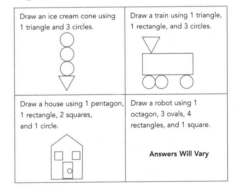

# Answer Key

## Page 66

1. Triangles cannot have two right angles. Right triangles are the only triangles that have a right angle. A right triangle has only one right angle.; 2. Their circles are the same size because the radius is half of the diameter.; 3. All angles of an octagon are obtuse.

## Page 67

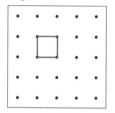
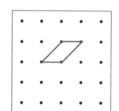
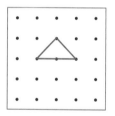
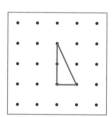

## Page 68

```
s l h j r x x q y h d q w c
n i u e e n d o t r o u x t
o o l l c o n g s b p a t o
g s r g t g o b q s j d j z
a e q n a y g u u c r r m x
x c c a l a q a w x i y w
e v f i g o t g r a g l u f
h f f r l p n c e i f a w e
h h g t e g e r o n v t r z
i x e m a c p n h l m e b k
z r t r a p e z o i d r l x
a z z y f v m v h f u a w h
z k d p k t c t h w i l t i
l p q e v i n h y z v s v j
```

## Page 69

1. cylinder; 2. rectangular prism; 3. cube; 4. sphere; 5. cone; 6. square pyramid; 7. Answers will vary. They may include the following: The figure is a square pyramid. It has 5 vertices, 8 edges, and 5 faces.; 8. Side A polygons are quadrilaterals. They are all closed polygons. Side B figures are not regular polygons. They are open figures and do not have parallel and congruent sides or angles.

## Page 70

9 - 3 =

6 + 3 =

# Answer Key

## Page 71

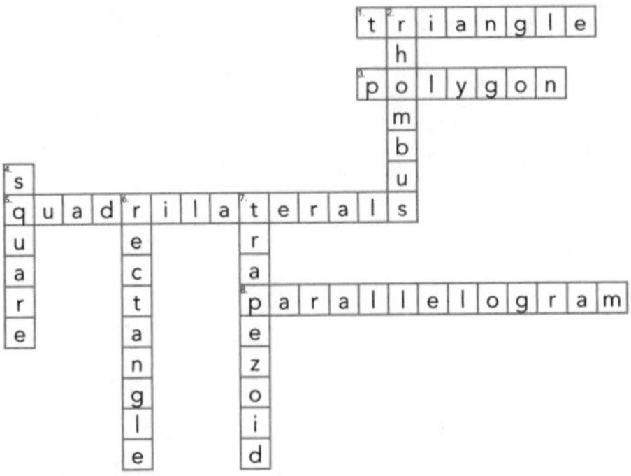

Crossword puzzle answers:

- triangle
- rhombus
- polygon
- square
- quadrilaterals
- rectangle
- trapezoid
- parallelogram

## Page 72

1. 1, 2, 3, 5, 6, 8, 9; 2. 4, 7 because they have no sides or corners